Affiliate Marketing Basics

Janet Smith

Copyright © 2014 Sandy Smith

All rights reserved.

ISBN-13: 978-1505429978

ISBN-10: 1505429978

DEDICATION

Dedicated to all online entrepreneurs

Affiliate Marketing Breakout

Disclaimer

Reasonable care has been taken to ensure that the information presented in this book is accurate. However, the reader should understand that the information provided does not constitute legal, medical or professional advice of any kind. No Liability: this product is supplied "as is" and without warranties. All warranties, express or implied, are hereby disclaimed. Use of this product constitutes acceptance of the "No Liability" policy. If you do not agree with this policy, you are not permitted to use or distribute this product. Neither the author, the publisher nor the distributor of this material shall be liable for any losses or damages whatsoever (including, without limitation, consequential loss or damage) directly or indirectly arising from the use of this product. Use at your own risk.

Contents

Using Clickbank as an Affiliate Marketing Career Launch Pad

Exploring Why There Is Ease in Starting Affiliate Marketing Ventures

Article Directories Really Help In Affiliate Marketing

Guidelines for Creating a Superior Affiliate Marketing Website

Income Increase Tips For Affiliate Marketers

Is It Possible To Pocket A Six Figure Income Through Affiliate Marketing?

Locating Top Affiliate Marketing Programs

Spam Complaints and How to Avoid Them in Affiliate Marketing

The Definition of Affiliate Marketing and What It Entails

The Effect That Blogging Has On Affiliate Marketing

The Importance of Mailing Lists in Affiliate Marketing

The Sure Way to Boost Your Niche Affiliate Marketing Business

Writing Quality Keyword Rich Articles for Affiliate Marketing

Using Link Building to Market Your Affiliate Website

Using Social Networking to Market Your Affiliate Site

Weekly, Bi-Weekly, Or Monthly: Which Affiliate Pay Structure Is Best

Using Clickbank as an Affiliate Marketing Career Launch Pad

Affiliate marketing is a viable way to make good income from commissions earned after selling products and services on behalf of a business. Many people have gone on to make impressive incomes from this activity having started from pretty humble beginnings. For the novice who wishes to get into affiliate marketing knowing where to start can be very challenging. Clickbank may just be your launch pad into this career if you are interested in dealing with information products. As one of the biggest information product marketplaces online Clickbank has proved to be a great affiliate marketing platform even for the novices in the trade. Clickbank deals in the purchase and sale of more than 30,000 information products. You can work on

Clickbank as either a vendor or an affiliate. As an affiliate you will be required to sell the informational products that the vendors have created. For the topic of discussion at hand we will consider what it takes to be an affiliate marketer on Clickbank. To start off you will have to register or sign up. Much like what happens in other websites you will be required to choose an ID that you will use every time you log in. with this ID in place you can now access the Clickbank marketplace and sample the products which you can sell. Clickbank have arranged the marketplace in categories of products which makes it easy for you to select that which you feel most likely to sell. You can choose a single item or several. Having selected the product(s) the next step will be to acquire a 'Hoplink' that will be used to direct prospective customers to the relevant vendor sales page. The 'Hoplink' takes the form of a HTML code which is only produced after your user ID is entered into a requisite form. Since each product that you want to sell has its own 'Hoplink' you may end up with quite a number. Clickbank affiliates usually file these hoplinks, sales page links, and product information for easy reference. To sell the Clickbank products that you have selected you just need to have the hoplinks input to the sales material. Being a vendor is not difficult either. You just need to have a product and pay an amount to have it listed on the marketplace. Before the product is sold it has to be Clickbank approved.

Exploring Why There Is Ease in Starting Affiliate Marketing Ventures

Unlike many other businesses where starting off is really hard affiliate marketing has some clear advantages that have made it very popular with many aspiring online entrepreneurs. This is one of the few businesses where you can start earning a respectable income even in the short term. Perhaps the greatest advantage there is to affiliate marketing has to do with the fact that there are ready products which you can start selling immediately. We all appreciate how difficult it is to come up with a new product and have it become successful such that you make a decent income from your creation. In affiliate marketing you choose to sell products that you are sure of being successful with and the range of these is large and varied. Many start-up businesses have a hard time when it comes to issues of collecting payments after sales are made. Affiliate marketers are not affected by this as their affiliate merchants do all the collection from the customers. In affiliate marketing each marketer is given an affiliate website by the merchant on whose behalf the marketing is being done. These websites are individually logged into such that all transactions which are made there are attributed to the affiliate marketer. There is no way that you can be denied of your dues. Affiliate marketing is all about marketing - period. As a marketer you are not concerned about inventories and stock taking and other intricacies of conventional businesses like delivery and shipping. Your task is just to sell the product and the merchant then assumes responsibility for getting the purchased item to the customer. The reach of affiliate marketing is most impressive. You can virtually sell products to any location on earth provided there is an internet connection. Unlike conventional businesses where the client base is restricted to a city or a country affiliate marketing means that the sales effort is global. With affiliate marketing you don't need to worry about trade restrictions that govern different countries. Some products especially the informational type only require that the customer has an internet connection and a computer for downloading purposes. One advantage that also stands out prominently has to do with the Internet itself. The internet is accessible 24-7-365 and by extension your affiliate marketing website also is. No matter where you are and regardless of the time you can always expect that someone somewhere can give you business.

Article Directories Really Help In Affiliate Marketing

Affiliate marketers have to be aware of all the resources at their disposal that they can use to their businesses advantage. Business advantage in this context refers to the ability of the venture to endear itself to both existent and prospective clientele.

Affiliate marketing begins from the choice of product that you want to sell. After selecting a product and a customer niche it is time to consider what tactics will be employed to generate sales page traffic. There are a couple of tactics that can be employed for this purpose including SEO and email marketing. The versatile affiliate marketer will however seek to employ a free tactic known as article marketing. Through article marketing many affiliate marketers have been able to gain significant traffic and pleasant compensating rewards to boot. Many affiliate marketers are taking up article writing and submission in cognizance of the benefits that can be accrued from doing so. Ready articles are submitted to article directories where they are published upon their satisfying of stated prerequisites. It is agreeable that not every marketer can be a talented writer especially when the article requires the insertion of particular keywords. In either case the affiliate marketer has a marketing job to take care of. He or she is better off hiring an article writer to do the job and then enjoy the increased volume of traffic for a very long time. With submission directories one ought to understand that they are already well placed in search engines. This is a huge boon for affiliate marketers and for good reason. An article that has been well prepared in terms of keyword insertion and density will undoubtedly be ranked highly which translates into more viewership. With increased viewership it is also very probable that this will be translated into sales. One thing that must be very clear about the writing of these articles is with regards to the content. The perfect article offers the reader much sought information about the product niche area and not the product itself per se. This is the information that the reader will go through and hopefully make a decision as to whether the product is worth buying. Articles that have been placed in directories have resource boxes where information about the affiliate marketer and the affiliate product sale website link is inserted. It is important to make the article details as interesting as possible to ensure that the reader goes all the way to the bottom where the resource box is.

Guidelines for Creating a Superior Affiliate Marketing Website

Your efforts as an affiliate marketer should be directed towards attracting online traffic to your website and not the vice versa. This is why the website you design for this effort should adhere to basic guidelines that are known to be traffic-friendly. Clarity, comprehension and consistence are the basic things that you would like your website to be known for. The visitor must be able to immediately have a clue as to what you have on offer as this will persuade him or her to read on. The website you have in mind should be designed to be appealing to the target prospective clientele. The term 'appealing' can be misconstrued to mean that the site should be full of visual effects and other like additions. In business, a website that is cumbersome to those trying to access it does not make the desired headway. It is best to have a website that will make a good impression from the onset. Choose your colors and fonts wisely as well as the tone of language

used. Ensure that you communicate with visitors in manner that will convince them to do business with you. Alongside the issues of relevance as have been mentioned above the website should be easy to use. While some degree of complexity is fine depending on the products and services that are being offered being extra complex is not advisable. What visitors appreciate most in a website is the quality of content. This is characteristic of some of the more successful websites we have around. While designing a website you should have the mindset of a customer whether he or she is a regular buyer or a prospect. The site should as much as possible make the visitor's experience pleasant for whatever that he or she wants to do. Pay particular attention to issues of ordering and item display. The website should not contain what you think is best for the traffic – the content should be informed by actual customer sentiments. A successful website combines excellent design with superb navigation. Navigation involves the use of links that lead to a web page where desired content is to be found. Links should therefore be well denoted so that a visitor can know where the click will lead to. Alongside navigation it is vital that a website is regularly updated. Access and download speeds are also critical to a website's popularity.

How to Choose the Best Affiliate Program

Before choosing any affiliate program you should research and discover the best and make use of the same by promoting them before your competitors hear about them. At the moment your competitors start to realize the current affiliate program, you should be already making money from the next killer product. The overall advantage of the best affiliate programs is that they help an individual to make more money online. Some affiliates select the wrong programs to promote which in most cases limits their ability to make a good income.

Basically there is no specific best affiliate marketing program but what you do all depends on the markets that you choose to get involved with. It is quite simple to choose the affiliate program in that out of the internet marketing an individual will find an opportunity to ride on the back of the product launch and the hype that it creates. When going through the sites such as Commission Junction among others, always look at the items that are selling the most and obtain the best. Such products already have a proven track record and will enable you have a better time spent in looking at different angles in order to attract buying traffic other than spending your time in testing the new affiliate offers so as to see whether or not they will convert as you may expect.

In most cases, the affiliate products and services offers that are selling the most also have the best sales pages as the site owner has already done comprehensive testing to achieve the best conversion rates he or she requires. It is always best to find the right traffic and send it elsewhere where you as an individual know your chances of making money are higher generally. An affiliate benefits in that he or she is

paid for each and every customer or client got through his or her effort. Any time a client purchases the service or product, portion of the profit got from that particular transaction is credited to the affiliates account. This is deposited as a commission. In most cases, the compensation amount is based on fixed value for each visit or every registration. When it comes to affiliate marketing, the merchant's benefits on a wider place to sell their services and goods which attracts very many customers thus, increased sales.

Income Increase Tips For Affiliate Marketers

Affiliate marketing has for some time been seen as the ultimate big-income-making career and it is this misperception that has really thrown many novices off balance. The fact of the matter is that there is no such career in existence and if there were then it would have already been out of bounds for very many. Like all other careers and jobs affiliate marketing is all about hard work and getting to learn the ropes step by step. This is the mantra that affiliate marketer novices ought to live by because the initial experience is far from the rosy picture that has been created of the trade. Indeed many people have quit their regular jobs and embarked on affiliate marketing.

While some have fared on really well some have been disillusioned by the high income mirage. In affiliate marketing there is no guaranteed way to follow so as to make the high income that is desired by many. The approach that one affiliate marketer adopts and becomes successful with is not necessarily the same one that another marketer will flourish with. Affiliate marketing is more of an individual approach because it is you who knows what your customers like through the correspondence you share. The approach that you use in the initially will definitely require some tweaking of sorts with regard to the realities on the ground. The business environment everywhere is highly dynamic and the most successful people are the ones who are ready to adapt to these changes by being innovative. It is all about understanding the demands and wishes of the traffic you encounter and then offering exactly what suits them.

Affiliate marketers cannot afford to be ignorant about integral details like latent syntax and SEO. Expert knowledge on the use of keywords and the manner in which they work is of essence. All these are critical to ensuring that search engines work to your advantage. Affiliate marketers rarely prosper without having their own websites and blogs. Here the importance of keyword phrases in creating content rich information again comes to the fore. Such are the basic things one needs to know if good income is to be made. Inasmuch as individual effort counts nothing beats experience. You learn so much more by referring from those who've been in the field longer. This is another way of saying that industry networking should also be taken seriously.

Is It Possible To Pocket A Six Figure Income Through Affiliate Marketing?

Generally the ones who own the websites and lack the products or the services of their own to market, it is always a hard task to earn money through the internet. It is possible to sell space for advertising but you have to attract several people to your site. You must attract big traffic in order to sell the advertising space. If you do not do so, you cannot be able to earn any money from anybody to let you advertise their sites. If you are scantly able to attract large traffic to your site and you do not have goods and services to sell, your solution is the six figure income program.

In the six figure income program, the author educates an individual on how to earn not less than one thousand dollars per day annually. The advantage of the six figure income program is that the author is ready to help an individual in every move he takes. Generally speaking, most marketers prefer to start earning money from home as a part time basis. Most of the websites depend on affiliate marketing to enable them gain a lot of sales since it is a simple concept. What affiliate marketing generally entails is selling of other people's goods and services for a commission which ranges between 5 to 25 percent of the product price. The secret is to convert the traffic to sales by making sure that the goods and services you are marketing on your own website target your visitors and target group. You should also ensure that your adverts do not look like conventional advertisements. This is so because many people do not take their time to pay attention to the banners that are scattered all over but they do visit your site for information on what you provide. When you are seeking for a product as an affiliate you need to look at some websites that sell the goods and services that are related to your website's information. Most of these websites contain affiliate programs and always have a link that is put on their site including the information on how an individual can sign up to join them as an affiliate. Basically, affiliate marketers always enjoy the luxury of being their own boss and they work in their own time.

Locating Top Affiliate Marketing Programs

Affiliate marketing programs abound in the internet and

if you are in the search of a good one then you will definitely be spoilt for choice. This is not a mere taunt; there are literally several thousands of options which you can explore. As with everything available online there are good and bad options when it comes to affiliate marketing programs. Some of the programs will work to your benefit and others won't be so helpful. The main consideration that many potential affiliate marketers are really concerned with is the amount of money that they stand to gain from their efforts. The commissions that these affiliate marketing programs offer is quite varied.

The highest paying programs offer as much as 20 to 25 percent on each product that is sold through a marketer's links. For such programs business can be really good since they characteristically sell products that are hugely popular across the globe. The second most important consideration that is used as a selection criterion by affiliate marketers has to do with the reputation that the program enjoys. You will definitely not go wrong with a program that is recognized the world over as being a market leader.

Customers on the other hand also look for brand names that they recognize. Being an affiliate marketer on a program like Western Union is bound to be successful from the get go purely because of the global recognition. Choose a program that enjoys many positive referrals because the task of converting these into sales won't be too difficult. Similar to the point just mentioned about the goodwill associated with a particular affiliate marketing program is the consideration about the products sold therein. A common characteristic that most of the top affiliate marketing websites share is the fact that they offer products that bear really popular brand names. Such brand names instill lots of confidence into prospective customers and even the already existing ones. It is undeniable that these products sell most and an affiliate marketer who offers such is definitely going to earn healthy returns. Affiliate marketing programs have different ways of dealing with their affiliates. An affiliate marketer will do much better working with a program that has pleasant earning incentives like commissions for product promotion via ads on the affiliate's website. Granted that joining many of these affiliate marketing programs is free it won't hurt if you try doing so.

Spam Complaints and How to Avoid Them in Affiliate Marketing

The successful affiliate marketer has a substantial subscriber list that he or she can rely upon for sustained business even in lean times. The tenets of affiliate marketing dictate that to maintain such a list there has to be communication between the two parties. The subscribers expect that you will be in regular contact with them by following up on their inquiries and comments. This communication is normally by means of email. Subscribers loath spam mail and as an affiliate marketer you should make sure that you do not get spam complaints from any of your subscribers. Spam is an issue that gives affiliate marketing a really bad name and you simply cannot allow this to ruin an otherwise vibrant venture.

There are simple things that you can do to ensure your business is spam complaint-free. To begin with you must pay attention to the credibility of the information that you provide your customers with. Whatever the format of information you offer them (this can be audio, video, or written) you should ensure that it is factual and reliable. For a business where you cannot usually make facial contact your credibility is measured upon the content you offer. For this matter you cannot afford to have haphazardly prepared material on your website. All that the subscribers read must let them know you are a reliable expert in the designated area. Customers place their confidence in the product or service you are selling simply because you said so. This statement might be valid but it doesn't at all mean that the customers will just purchase anything. The fact of the matter is that the Internet is also host to a very big number of bogus products and not all prospective customers are gullible enough to be swayed into purchasing such. As the affiliate marketer you are expected to have done your market research well in advance to avoid ending up with egg on your face. You will need to personally vet the products you are selling so as to make an informed recommendation to the customers. Staying focused on the job is an issue that is critical to any business let alone affiliate marketing. With focus you will be consistently diligent even in the tiniest of details. Businesses grow with time if the working standards are maintained highly. With this at the back of your mind your affiliate marketing venture will not be a disappointment.

The Definition of Affiliate Marketing and What It Entails

Increased business competition on a global scale has soared to unprecedented rates particularly in the last few years. Each and every business has an intention of achieving economies of scale and this is mainly done through a reduction of costs wherever possible. Marketing is the means by which businesses get their products into the customer realm. It is the means through which prospective clients are sensitized about the availability of products that they need or which they may need. Marketing is not a cheap effort especially when you consider the media through which it is done. Of late many businesses have been using the Internet as a marketing medium. Affiliate marketing is one of the forms through which this is done and it has proved to be both cheap and effective. In affiliate marketing the concerned business has an affiliate(s) whose work it is to lead customers toward the said business. The business then rewards its affiliates for every client that was landed thanks to the efforts of the affiliates. A business may have affiliates in the form of management companies, affiliate managers, and affiliate networks. It is these affiliates who conduct internet marketing on behalf of the business and in so doing promote the goods and services that they offer. Affiliate marketers have some chosen tools of trade that they utilize in the marketing effort. Some of the more common techniques largely used in affiliate marketing include Search Engine Optimization (SEO), search engine marketing, and email marketing. In the formative days of this marketing technique goods and services were often promoted by means of spam. This has however changed to the creation of web pages. The web pages are optimized for search engine ranking through the use of niche keywords. An optimized web page will undoubtedly lead to more site traffic and thus the service or product being promoted will be exposed to a greater audience. Getting enough traffic for a constructed website can be pretty challenging. It is the SEO techniques that are mostly used in ensuring that more and more people are made aware about the website. Affiliate marketing is yet to achieve its full potential but its popularity is on the rise especially after the marketers started refraining from using spam. The advantages of affiliate marketing are however very real when you consider the minimal costs involved, the global audience, and the short time span required to get the word around.

The Effect That Blogging Has On Affiliate Marketing

Before we get into the nitty-gritty details of how blogging affects the affiliate marketing effort it is necessary that to understand what these two terminologies entail. This is especially for the sake of those who are still green in such matters. Blogging is the action of using a blog otherwise known as a web log. As the latter name suggests blogs are journal-like online forums where people post entries which are then sequentially ordered. Many blogs are dedicated to particular topic categories though there are some on which any topic can be discussed. Affiliate marketing involves the online promotion of the goods and services produced by given business. A business that owns a website needs to have people traffic who can then be convinced to buy. The affiliate marketing effort is done by individuals on behalf of the business and these persons are termed to be 'affiliates'. Affiliates use a combination of techniques to push the promotion agenda. Some of these techniques are the use of web links, search engine optimization, and through networks.

Affiliates receive compensation from the business as per the traffic they have directed to the website. Blogs have steadily gained much popularity and both affiliate marketers and web developers have been quick to take advantage of this fact. Using blogs as forums for advertisement and promotion is a trend that affiliates are now embracing in addition to the others mentioned previously. Web developers have made things better by introducing online blog software that facilitates more convenient access to businesses via the affiliates. Thanks to this software 'quack' affiliates whose intentions are to defraud and scam can now be blocked. This has greatly enhanced the credibility of affiliate marketing. Blogging has contributed in a large way to the success of affiliate marketing as a means of online promotion.

Through the use of keywords search engines are more capable of leading interested people to the relevant websites. Unlike spamming which is frowned upon blogging is not as offensive. A popular blog is visited by very many people in a short time span and by so doing a product or service is marketed to quite a big audience. With an audience drawn from all over the globe many businesses have experienced an upsurge in customer volume and of course bottom-lines have drastically improved. Affiliate marketing on blogs makes use of keywords to direct traffic. Videos and photos are some of the additional techniques that are used to capture the attention of prospective clients.

The Importance of Mailing Lists in Affiliate Marketing

Mailing lists are advantageous in several ways. The best thing about having a mailing list is that an individual is able to automate a lot of the process by the use of an auto responder. This is a service that is offered online and it handles the mailings and the mail lists on your behalf for a small fee that is paid on a monthly basis. The other services include the get response and a webmaster will also give an individual access to form a simple detail that appears on his or her website. It normally asks the visitors the e-mail address and their names. This enables an individual to entice the visitors to sign up by providing a free report in exchange for the information. It prompts them to become the members of your mailing list automatically. The mailing list's importance to the marketer is significant. Some marketers have thousands of names on their mailing lists and anytime a new product is introduced to the market, the super marketers have the inside track on the sales using their ability to contact their other members.

Numerous people take interest in affiliate marketing as a way of earning a living or to earn supplementary income. The affiliate marketing growth is not a difficult task to understand since it provides a way to help in making money from retail products without having to stock inventory, or handle returns in the event that the client is not happy with the product or make credit sales to the public. When it comes to affiliate marketing, the sales process is entirely hands off. When there is no work to be carried out along the lines of making direct sales, there may be a lot of work involved in making the public aware of the goods and services you are promoting to them. There are two ways by which you can bring out your products to the public. One is by purchasing pay per click advertising on the main search engines. You can also do this by building a website promoting single or several products. Research reveals that current purchasers are likely to purchase in coming days. This is because it is quite simpler to make a sale to a proven customer than to attract a new client.

The Sure Way to Boost Your Niche Affiliate Marketing Business

Owning a website has proven to be arguably one of the most effective ways to establish a vibrant niche affiliate marketing business. With this reality there are many considerations that budding affiliate marketers take to mind and most of these have to do with the constrained budgets that they stick to. To own a website you don't have to break the bank – at least not until you explore all the options that are in your realm. Purchasing a website is one of the most viable options that niche affiliate marketers have at their disposal.

The costs of acquiring a ready-made website notwithstanding, the realities of the times are such that such an asset can be bought at very friendly prices. In considering the cost of such an acquisition you have to weigh the relevance of the design to your marketing effort. Ensure that these two aspects complement each other even before you start negotiating. The second consideration has to do with the content on the website. You must ensure that it is all very originally unique – not some mere copy-paste job. Purchasing such a website comes with very handy advantages. Firstly, it is important to appreciate that we are all talented in different fields. As an affiliate marketer you may not be able to craft a website on your own and even if you do it might not be as impressive as what a professional in the area can achieve.

The other advantage you will savor is the fact that a ready website will enable you to start marketing right away. As an extension to what has been said on specialization the website will enable you to do that which you do best – marketing – immediately. A ready-made website sees to it that your business downtime is not too prolonged. There are things that you must also check for when making such a purchase. You should be knowledgeable enough to identify a niche affiliate marketing website that you can adopt seamlessly. The content in the website must be ascertained for originality and here online software like Copyscape becomes really handy. You can't just buy blindly – check the seller's background to be sure about his or her credibility. The expenses that you incur in this endeavor may seem to be prohibiting at the onset but with a useful website in place for your customers you will definitely enjoy business sooner rather than later.

Writing Quality Keyword Rich Articles for Affiliate Marketing

The use of keywords in article writing is mainly for the purpose of achieving top ranking in the various search engines. It would seem that if keywords are the means to getting best ranking then saturating articles with these phrases would be the winning approach. This is not the case since doing so has been known to result in undesired results upon scouring the search engines. The reason why this happens is due to the webmaster-developed algorithms which determine those articles that are filled with relevant content and those that are not. The practice currently is to have articles whose keyword content makes about 12 percent of the total word volume. Articles that are deemed to have surpassed these stipulations are often faced with the risk of being banned.

Affiliate marketers who require SEO articles need not worry since there are plenty of talented writers across the globe who are capable of inserting the right number of keywords into an article while ensuring that the content is informative and seamless. The basic guidelines for writing SEO articles therefore all have to do with how the required phrase distribution is done. An ideal scenario is to have one or two keywords in both the starting and ending paragraphs. All the paragraphs in between these two should have at least one keyword depending on the length of the article. This may however be quite tricky when the desired keyword is hard to insert by virtue of its wording arrangement. In such scenarios article writers are normally offered the convenience of using both singular and plural forms of the same. While writing keyword rich articles it is advisable to keep reading the article as it develops and upon its completion. This is to ensure that coherence is maintained. The best articles are the ones that keep the reader engaged from top to bottom in a way that they don't seem to notice the repeated phrases. Then again it is possible that the keywords are well distributed but the core content isn't informative. Such an article may pass the algorithm test but will certainly flop with the readers thus affecting the sales negatively. Regardless of the difficulty that may be present when using keywords it will be counterproductive to force the phrase just anywhere. This affects the whole article as understanding the content becomes difficult. Again this is a good reason to hire a professional SEO article writer. They do charge some money but this is easily recouped from the sales that result.

Using Link Building to Market Your Affiliate Website

Several owners of online business mainly the ones who lack whole internet marketing background have a clear marketing plan that obtaining a large number of links for their websites is a beneficial factor. In real sense, getting back the links when done wrongly automatically kills the website. There are several ways to put back the killed links to an individual's online website. Article marketing has great advantages over other methods of link building. Other websites owners also find links by forwarding their sites to numerous link directories. If you have a large number of links online, its just like a guarantee for most search engines to get your links and find their way to your website. Some online business owners post their links on forums and blogs in order to get clients.

These forums are quite better ways of building links. This is so because it allows the business owner to connect and bond with other people on the internet. Other people will see, view and respond to the comments. They can also surf on your website and see what you offer on it. The method can be time consuming since it takes too much time to post the forums and blogs. But it also takes a lot of time for other people to forget your online website. Some people prefer article marketing as the best compared to other links in that article marketers most of the time gives them room to get their marketing over all other link building fast. Through writing good articles, the readers view them and find the knowledge or the information that they will have to share with others. For them to find more, they can just pay attention to the links in the bio boxes about the authors and visit the publisher websites.

Apart from quality traffic and high rankings, article marketing is also highly scalable. There is a great cumulative effect as many articles keep on being submitted and approved by the article directories. If article writing is carried out thoroughly for some few weeks, readers will read and believe the writers as they can see for themselves the dedication efforts that are usually put by the article marketers – credible information is the winning effort. Here an individual now has several channels. The article marketers know how to use this method to let other individuals view them as experts in that particular field.

Using Social Networking to Market Your Affiliate Site

Social networking is one of the methods of affiliate marketing strategies which can help you to sell more affiliate products and services online. The affiliate business based at home can be used to gain a variety of best affiliate marketing strategies which are mostly used online. Website promotion, banner advertisements, search engines and email marketing among others are all based on affiliate marketing business though there are networking websites which can also be taken as part strategies for the home based affiliate business. Social networking is the cheapest and simplest home based affiliate marketing business strategy option that is readily available. Advertising your home based affiliate marketing business is another top affiliate marketing strategy on the internet that can be run easily. Social networking sites are essentially online places when you can meet with your clients. Generally, most social networking websites are based on particular subjects and they encourage those who share same interests in specific topics in order to get together to discuss the relevant issues, provide advice and ask questions among others.

These social networking sites are able to focus on any topic. They can also focus on subjects such as politics, television shows, bands, jobs, current events, and hobbies or ant imaginable topic. The affiliate marketer is able to take advantage of the social networking site in order to reach a target audience without spending money. Working at home has become increasingly popular and there are numerous websites which focus on this particular subject. There are also several networking sites which are focused and devoted to the topic of working at home. Here the parties who are interested in this particular topic can take the home based affiliate marketing opportunity in order to post a link to his website when it offers a valuable thing to the conversation. This is best since the social networking site feature on a high concentration of an individual's targeted group. When it comes to social networking site to promote home based affiliate marketing businesses, it is crucial to ensure that you are following the regulations associated with the social marketing sites. The social networking sites at times may have restrictions regarding the posting of links and failure to abide by the set restrictions may make you be barred from the social networking sites. Because of this, anyone who is interested in using these sites should read the user agreement to ensure that they are not violating any rule.

Weekly, Bi-Weekly, Or Monthly: Which Affiliate Pay Structure Is Best?

When looking for an affiliate program that is going to be right for your internet enterprise it can be hard at times. This is because of the incredibly many affiliate programs that are offered on the internet. First of all you should ensure that the affiliate program is credible and has gotten good results for other companies.

You need to ask if the program offers residual earnings. This kind of gain is got from earnings and is considered as payments issued monthly from every sale. If you find a product that you are ready to promote and it's from another merchant search the internet for similar affiliate sourced products. Know what the program offers, and you continue to supply specific rates. This offers an individual with good information of the sales that he or she is going to get for a specific good.

Try and select a program that offers promotional resources because it is simpler to promote an item if there are banners, sites and adverts that are given at no further cost. It can also make your promotion activities more graceful and a lot simpler than you never expected. Consider the program that offers a good pay structure; try to get information concerning the way the affiliate program performs. If you are even the smallest bit confused, then you should shift to the program option. Affiliate programs should always be in a position to make it right just how their particular program performs.

Do not choose a program which will require you to spend anything or needs you to store some products. As an affiliate, you become part of the corporation's sale force but you're employed only on commission and should not hold inventory. Come up with the leads for your affiliate by employing e-mail newsletters. An internet site is very crucial mostly when you are planning to generate more cash. Read up on a way to build a work-at-home business and what's required to achieve success. This can sound a very critical point to you if this is your very first time trying it out. Prioritize the factors concerned in affiliate programs. When you follow simple steps, these questions can become a lot simpler to get answers to, and finding the affiliate program right for your internet business will be easy.

www.ingramcontent.com/pod-product-compliance
Lightning Source LLC
Chambersburg PA
CBHW021042180526
45163CB00005B/2240